I'm going to be an...

ENGINEER

AUTUMN
PUBLISHING

Written by Marnie Willow
Illustrated by Junissa Bianda
Additional artwork by Hazel Quintanilla

Designed by Lee Italiano
Edited by Helen Catt

Copyright © 2020 Igloo Books Ltd

Published in 2021
First published in the UK by Autumn Publishing
An imprint of Igloo Books Ltd
Cottage Farm, NN6 0BJ, UK
Owned by Bonnier Books
Sveavägen 56, Stockholm, Sweden

Manufactured in China. 0721 001
10 9 8 7 6 5 4 3 2 1

Library of Congress Cataloging-in-Publication
Data is available upon request.

ISBN 978-1-80022-863-4
autumnpublishing.co.uk
bonnierbooks.co.uk

I'm going to be an...

ENGINEER

AUTUMN PUBLISHING

When I grow up,

I'm going to be an
engineer!

I'll start by drawing my design on paper. Then I'll build a model to test it out, before bringing it to life!

I'll take cars apart, tune them up, oil them down,
then put them back together
so they move...

... like
GREASED LIGHTNING!

I'll design buildings and skyscrapers that everyone will know. They'll be famous all over the world.

I'll build long bridges over giant rivers.

(No more swimming with sharks!)

I'll do
incredible
sums to make
sure my creations
are safe and
strong.

I'll count higher and
higher than ever before.
They'll have to invent
a whole new number
just for me.

There are machines **everywhere**,
and I'll engineer them all.

Maybe I'll make a
machine that
Granny can use

to **whizz**
to the shops.

Or I'll invent a clever hospital machine that spots the early signs...

... of spotty-dotty, green-and-grotty snot-and-goo disease.

Some of
my machines
will fly!

They'll swoop and dive and slice through the sky...

... faster than any bird.

Others will dive deep underwater.

I'll study how sea creatures swim so well and make a clever copy—a marvelous mix of sockets and screws with flippers and fishy fins.

I won't stop there.
My machines will go up into **space**.

Just watch me go!

A special beeping **satellite** and a **rocket** that flies...

... to the

DARK SIDE OF THE MOON.

Or even further: machines on Mars!
I'll build rovers and buggies,
space suits and solar panels...

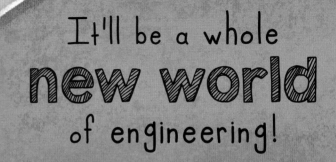

It'll be a whole **new world** of engineering!

When I grow up,
I'll do all these things.

But I've got lots of other things to do first.

BEING AN
ENGINEER

Nearly everything made by people has been designed by an engineer, from your washing machine to the building you live in. Engineers use math and science to make things work. They draw designs on graph paper or on computers, and often make mini models to test how well their designs work.

There are lots of different types of engineers. Some invent machines that help people walk or find new ways to heal sick people. Others design bridges and buildings. Some make cars, planes, or even spaceships. Who knows what you'll create?